SURVIVING OR LIVING

ANNE RAE

Surviving or Living

Copyright © 2025 by Anne Rae.

All rights reserved. No part of this publication may be reproduced, distributed, or transmitted in any form or by any means, including photocopying, recording, or other electronic or mechanical methods, without the written consent of the publisher. The only exceptions are for brief quotations included in critical reviews and other noncommercial uses permitted by copyright law.

MILTON & HUGO L.L.C.
4407 Park Ave., Suite 5
Union City, NJ 07087, USA

Website: *www. miltonandhugo.com*
Hotline: *1- 888-778-0033*
Email: *info@miltonandhugo.com*

Ordering Information:
Quantity sales. Special discounts are granted to corporations, associations, and other organizations. For more information on these discounts, please reach out to the publisher using the contact information provided above.

Library of Congress Control Number:	2025901748
ISBN-13: 979-8-89285-435-1	[Paperback Edition]
979-8-89285-436-8	[Hardback Edition]
979-8-89285-437-5	[Digital Edition]

Rev. date: 01/23/2025

Contents

In pain 1
Healing 89
Feeling Alive 167

In pain

I allowed you to hurt me for so long
I forgot how my voice sounded
How strong my mind was
I was hiding in a body
overtaken by fear & guilt

Today my therapist asked what I want
My answer differing from others makes me ill
However
I want to see a bottle of pills &
not wonder how many it would take to kill
I want to wake up in the morning not wondering if I'm under the hill
I want to look in the mirror & not fear the reflection
I want to close my eyes &
not hear the worlds misconceptions
I want to lay down without grabbing my bones
I want to think about more than the unknown
I want to look at my skin & not be ashamed
I want to feel alive she exclaimed

I have lived
a quarter of my life
& my tank is on the darkness E

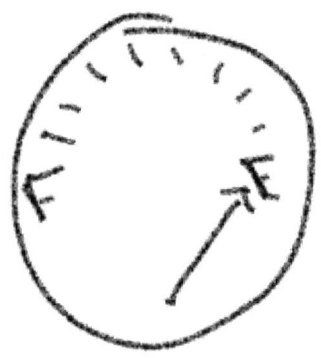

If asked to describe myself in one word
I'd say misunderstood
like the black sheep of the herd
There is so much I have yet to understand
please forgive me
as I have been under someone else's command

You turn your lamp on
& still choose to focus on
the dark

I learned at a young age
I never wanted to be
the spotlight on stage

I am your mother
four words that haunt me like no other
you believe my emotions & thoughts are given
that's why I keep so much hidden
your comments trapped inside my brain
they have brought so much pain

tension in the air
fear in our veins
typical high school day

The girl sighed
what's my purpose

She stated aloud

The odd thing was no one was around
It's as if the girl didn't want an answer

Your voice & ego
so chaotic & bold
how could I ever
expect you to hold
a mature conversation

I have hope
hope that one day there won't be
a blade by the bed
hope that one day I'll feel understood & well read
hope that one day a question
won't send me into a spiral
hope that one day with my kids
I'll break the toxic cycle
hope that one day I'll feel content
hope that one day I'll be my own safety net
hope that one day you'll realize
you're worth in other's eyes
hope that one day I'll live with no despise

her body told an unwritten story

skimmed over by many

understood by one

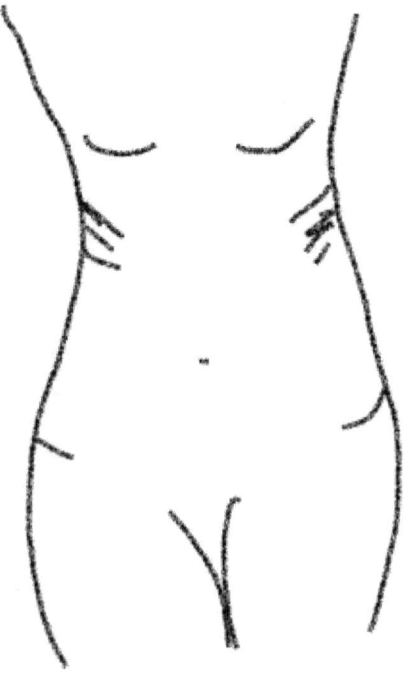

I've never felt I belong
I've never had four walls feel like home
I've never outweighed the bad with the good
I've never looked at the glass half full
I've gone days without feeling real
My therapist says overtime I'll heal

My life purpose has always
been unclear
It's left my overthinking brain
in immense fear
events emotions & regrets
are always so intense
normal has never been my end goal
I just want to be functional

all I asked you for
was to prepare me
all you have done
is scare me

I can't allow you to hurt me anymore
The leash and harness are on the floor
Your emotions so heavy & bold
How come I was always first to fold
I'll never be perfect in your eyes
It's taken me so long to realize

I'm still your mother she says
after telling lies about my life
I'm still your mother she says
While her voice makes me run and hide
I'm still your mother she says
As her words like blades leave scars behind
I'm still your mother she says
While being crowned villain of my life
I'm still your mother she says
As this love feels like a rotating knife
I'm still your mother she says
While I'm no longer your daughter she replies

My heart grew roots in you

The day will continue without you
It will shine differently though

It's okay
not to have
100 reasons
to stay
you just
need one

How can such a quick moment
be thought about for so long

we were in love one day
the next you threw it all away
you gave no reason
allowing our love to only
last for one season

Don't be so mean to yourself
You hold yourself back from opportunities
Because you believe the harsh things you say

What has happened to love
It makes me sad to see
so many broken hearts

You sit in a room
With so many people around you
& nothing
You feel alone

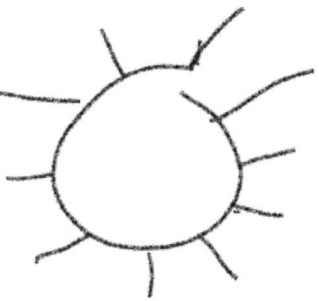

I dread the cold winter season
I could give 100 different reasons
but if we didn't get the cold, we wouldn't appreciate
the warm days

Sometimes
when we need someone else
we often just need to be okay
with being by ourselves

You don't have to stay in that small town
You can go somewhere that doesn't
make you frown

Sometimes no answer is the answer
You must understand that

I would love to be optimistic but
my eyes have a blue filter over them

You scared me so much
I stopped living
I have so much anger towards you for that

Your blood poison
it worries me it's in mine
You're the last thing I want to be

I'm haunted by your voice
as I lie awake tossing & turning in bed
The clock sounds another hour past
& I'm still replaying the simple yet evil hello
that left your mouth

hello

I gave my all
while loving you
You gave nothing
Leaving me more broken
than how you found me

Why wasn't I enough for you

I say to myself in bed for the
hundredth time

Learn from the uncomfortable times

She kissed him
His lips didn't taste how she imagined

You moved on so fast
Throwing my things in a box labeled the past

I hold on while you push me away
It breaks my heart that I wasn't good enough
to make you stay

What if there's a day our love only
exists on these pages

[handwritten note: you is me]

Maybe you knew the outcome the whole time

I relive days in my head
like I'll have the chance someday

Drinking is more than sips out of a glass
drinking is hoping the time will pass
Hoping you never feel again
I drink to numb at all
I drink to blur the past
Drinking is hoping the time will pass
Passing time leads to new time
New urges are pushing me to the blade
I know the scars will fade
There is no need to be afraid
Pain is growth... so they say
But what if the blade does not bring pain
Yet a numbness so inhumane

how
can
we
be
lost
in
a
moment
we
don't
want
to
be
in

Unsure when we'll see each other
I still think of you like an older brother
I'll never see your glasses
Hear your laugh
Or see your smile
I think a part of me will always be in denial
I have questions every day
If I got the chance
there would be so much to say
Often I panic thinking I forgot your voice
Would you do it again if you had the choice

The loneliness grew thick & dark
overtime after you left

Your hand in control of the
strings tied around my body

The hardest time to leave is
when you have no new home to go to
You leave with everything in hand
Tears rolling down to your chin
All with no destination

I wonder if my purpose is to show others love
I never get the same love reciprocated
It's nice to know I have a purpose though

You wanted an explanation & whether I told you
or not was very hard to decide
Because some of me does want
to tell you all the hell you have caused me
But more of me knows to keep it to myself &
walk away

You live swallowed by your ego
How miserable

We were a family of four controlled by one
I'm not sure family is the right word
but there were four of us

Your reaction so dramatic & bold
we stopped telling you the truth
& fed you with lies

- I am not evil
- okay

You asked about my pain
& said how could this happen to me
How much more selfish could you be

Control is out of your hands
& your voice lost

If you were satisfied with yourself
like you say you are
then you wouldn't be in everyone's business

If someone makes you question our love
leave
I want love that is undeniable &
has no room for hesitation

If I drew pain
It would look like you

My Christmas list?
The scars to go away by my wrist
Meet someone not labeled with the word caution
Start clean with my reputation
Be comfortable with hugs
Not end every reply in shoulder shrugs
a new perspective
& meds that are effective

There will be sad days ahead
There will be days you'd rather stay in bed
There will be days you cry yourself to sleep
There will be days you cut too deep
There will be days people disappoint you
There will be days you miss the social cues

Why did I have to shape myself to fit you

We drifted so far apart
I can't remember what you last touched

How can you not remember
When
Your words are in stone in my mind

I gave you my all
you dropped my heart &
watched it fall

You took a piece of my heart with you
You haven't been back since

I have given you twenty one years
You had your chances

Did I imagine it all
Was it all in my head
You left as if nothing was real

Maybe our flame was put out
so we didn't have a chance to burn down a whole city

I question if I'll be alone
with myself forever

Her biggest fear was becoming
that version of herself
Locked away on the highest shelf
a miserable, depressed, hopeless piece of her heart
Sits there often viewed as beautiful art
It has the power to kill
Running off pain, anger and manic thrill
One small mistake and it's here for a season
I can't allow this to be the beast awakening reason

Being seen was her biggest fear
& what she wanted most at the same time

She was always thinking about
what was happening next she never focused
on the moment in front of her
She missed it all

The most significant person belittled her
the whole time
She never had a chance

She shouldn't have been treated that way
But she "chose" to stay
Emotions tangled & abused
Her lip & skin bruised
Tomorrow's out of sight
She lost the fight

I waited so long for you
all that time wasted

Sometimes I'm comforted by the darkness
It's an odd feeling

Two people can be in love
But it just takes one to break it

& in two seconds she felt her heart drop
& break into a million pieces

That's the thing
we don't know much of
our life we've lived

An ordinary hot summer day
Ended with you passing away
Your choice haunts me at night
Your mind lying to you about what's right
You're mentioned often
You always will be

The voices screaming at strangers
help I'm in danger

Infinite miles between you & I
I hold back my tears trying not to cry
So much has changed since that day
The grass became gray
Winter days stinging bitter cold
Your exit was so permanent & bold

It was supposed to be us against the world

We lay in bed & I feel alone

I see a light at the end
of the tunnel
what awaits beyond there
I'm unsure
when I'll reach it
is unclear
however
there is comfort
knowing the end is near

Healing

My therapist and I were talking
about how I feel one bad moment
or day takes away the progress I've made

She assured me that no progress
can be taken away

I realize that as I am climbing
this mountain called life
there are going to be moments where
I set up my tent for the night

I don't lose anything
I remain where I am with my progress alongside me

You're the only one who can see your vision

You can ask the question &
process the answer or
you can continue to think about
the worst scenario
It's up to you

Maybe you're the reason someone
believes pure souls still exist

My actions have reason
I'm not a monster

If you loved the wrong one
that much
imagine how much you'll love the right one

There was a sparkle in the rain that day
The lightning brighter that night
The thunder sounding euphoric
-July 7th

I can't allow myself to fall down
when I've worked so hard
learning how to stand up

Sometimes there is no plan to follow
You have the opportunity to do whatever you want
There's no right or wrong just what makes sense to you

Maybe you're lost in a moment, but it's still
where you're supposed to be

She couldn't help but take things
personal since they were happening to her

She wanted to hate him
How couldn't she after he lead her astray
& played a stupid game
Maybe I should rephrase that
She was disappointed with him but thankful with what she was left with
She was the healthiest version of herself mentally & physically
& that's all she's ever wanted
She's fighting to keep herself
She never thought it would be possible

Flowers are beautiful
Sunsets are beautiful
Artwork is beautiful
Mountains are beautiful
Words are beautiful
All described with the same word yet nothing alike
Everything holds beauty

My soul aches for young love
Love that gives you butterflies
Love that holds no lies
Love that others admire
Love so passionate
it could never expire
Love that stays young forever

I am proud of myself

That feels so odd to say

Nonetheless a feeling
I want to experience
more often

If someone else did what you do
Would it impress you?

Stop labeling qualities bad & just accept them

She didn't care about sex
She wanted a soul connection
She wanted public affection
She wanted to be loved on the ugly days
She wanted a man to stay

he says what I have always wanted to hear

to some distance
is a reason to &
to others it's
an excuse not to

You tried shaping me to fit you
Cutting my body & mind to fit yours

My voice came out of your mouth for so long

You feel how you feel
If you weren't meant to
you wouldn't feel it
accept it & continue

It is unfair
that what holds
the most beauty
is inside of us

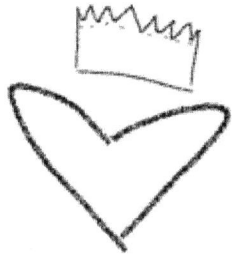

what she was waiting for was unclear
but she knew there had to be more

when you're 100%
on your own
no one can take away from you
all there is to do is add on

When you're lost in the moment
take a step back &
look at the bigger picture

you must allow yourself
to let go
you must allow yourself
the chance to grow

Fire is fire
No matter how you touch it
It burns you

You questioned my opinion for so long
I began forming it to fit you

stop allowing yourself
to drown in moments
you can stand up

If you wouldn't listen to their advice
why listen to their negative comments

If you're not putting in effort
to change
you're choosing to stay
where you are

what you're lacking
or unfulfilled with
can be changed by you

you'll see the progress in time
you must be patient &
willing to continue
while their is no visible change

thank you for taking
the time to explain it to me

open your heart & ears
you are loved
you are valued
you are intelligent
you are not consumed
you are where you are
your story is amazing
continue for the rest of us

Every negative needs a positive to function

You hold so much power & ability
to change
but you're too scared to move on

Please love the broken parts
They can still heal

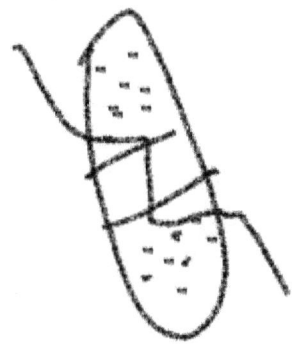

It's winter &
the flowers are still alive

why would I share
my bright ideas
with someone
who only sees gray

the negatives don't have to
negatively define you

& suddenly she thought
I can love myself the way
I want to love someone else
she focused on the little things
how she smiled at strangers
how cleaning before bed made her enjoy the mornings
how connected she felt while writing
she had fallen in love with herself & life

you can live in fear &
you can stay right here
Or
you can grow &
get away from the snow

If you continuously
let down by others do it yourself

one day I'll be quick to name
off my positive qualities
one day I'll stop waiting for others apologies
one day you'll understand your mind
one day you'll believe you're not behind
one day we'll be content
one day we'll live in the moment

There will come a day
you do things in silence
There will come a day
your life isn't ran by a substance
There will come a day
you feel whole
There will come a day
you're at peace with your soul

in a
world
full
of lies
listen
with
your
eyes

why should someone listen to you
if you don't listen to yourself
why should someone respect you
if you don't respect yourself
why should someone get to know you
if you don't know yourself

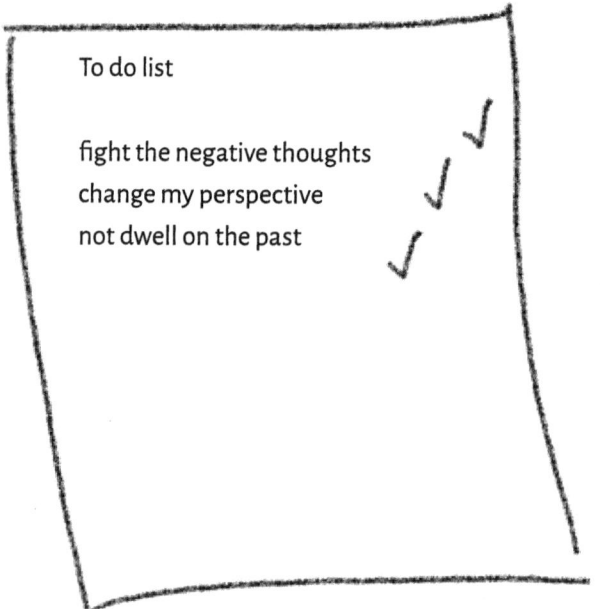

may your favorite person
never be hiding behind a disguise

while you water
your flowers
don't forget you
need water too

sometimes
we must go mute
so others can be seen

Don't force what doesn't fit

There is no timeline to your life just time

Why are you waiting for something
that can't happen without you

Understand your reaction to the situation
is all that's in your control

Sometimes while writing
I think the pencil leads me

Don't let the negative "what if's" control your life

& suddenly the darkness got quiet

Thank you for absorbing my problems
when I couldn't hold them alone

More than anything
the girl wanted to be
someone's first choice

I want someone who can accept my anxiety
Along with my stubborn mentality
I want someone who will take care of my heart
I want someone who will look at my body like it's art
I want someone who can empathize for others
I want someone who accepts why I'm not close with my mother
I want someone who thinks I'm as beautiful as the stars in the sky
I want someone who doesn't lie

You made my quiet, anxious voice
bold & opinionated
thank you

You're hands on my body
You're touch feels so natural
You're food for my soul

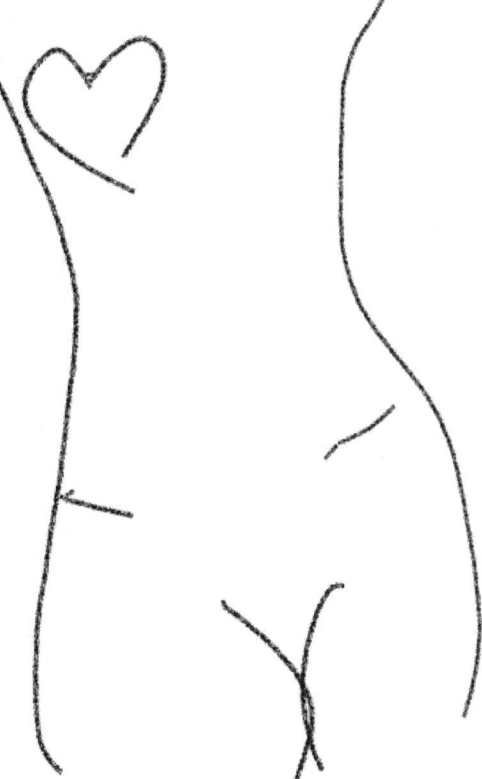

What do you want to talk about
What are you worried about

Her therapist asked

The girl hesitated in panic
as if she'll jinx herself
I think I feel content for once
She said

How refreshing
when you left
so did the clouds

If you're always searching for
the next thing when will
you ever feel satisfied?

Now that my days aren't black & grey
I'm upset I have let so much time slip away
I feel a purpose inside of me
I am alone & still have company
My voice mine & free
A life I have fought so hard to achieve

He made me feel smart
He made me feel understood
He made me feel powerful
He made me feel beautiful

I want to be in love
I want to be in a relationship
I want to be
but I don't have to be
I trust my time is coming

& then she understood loving herself
wasn't as hard as everyone made it seem

For so long I believed your twisted lies
It's like I was hypnotized
when you looked me in my eyes

You won't always get to know why
& that's okay because knowing why
won't change their actions

Your mental illness doesn't make loving you difficult
Don't blame yourself it's not your fault
It's okay to be upset that to others It's invisible
Some days getting out of bed feels impossible
The right people won't make you feel ashamed
There will come a day you feel your emotions are tamed

Feeling Alive

Someone will love your sensitive mind
Someone will think you're one of a kind
Someone will value your time
Someone will say "thank God she's mine"
Someone will buy you flowers
Someone will admire you for hours

how beautiful is it
that one day what
excites you most
you'll get to share
what the one you love

learn to adapt the favorite
qualities you search for in others

My soul aches for redemption
My mind craves direction
My body wants sensation
My voice screams for attention

their breath slowly sinking
their eyes looking into each other souls
about to become one

knowing your strengths & weaknesses
will benefit your relationships
understand & value what you have to offer

let's stay in
bed today

she said aloud
while rolling over

he was nodding
smiling back

you'll never know what you're capable of
If you don't leave your comfort zone

the good thing is your comfort zone
will always be there for you

they felt butterflies
sitting in silence
may their love
stay young forever

do you prefer a coloring book
or a blank sketchbook

I think you can learn a lot
about a person based on their answer

your smile so bright
your heart so kind
your words so healing
thank you

he made her feel wanted

it was a feeling she has
craved her whole

you're stronger than you know

there is a survivor in you

he brought colors into her life
that she had never seen before

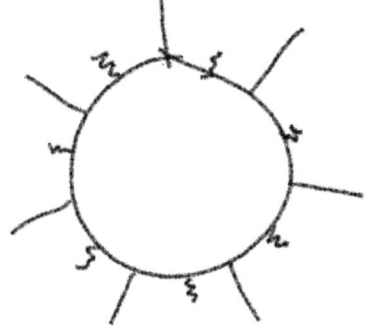

their souls intertwined
their hearts satisfied
their intentions pure

he showed her love
in so many ways
she began loving herself

my body
inexperienced
with your touch
yet aches for it

your intellectual thoughts
undress me effortlessly

How beautiful is it
that we share the same sky moon & stars

Maybe we'll get everything we ask for
or maybe we'll get more

It's your time to be selfish
Don't miss it

There is no incorrect way to live

You still have time to love your life

There will come a day you feel in place
Look around at your environment
see where you belong

I want you to myself
I am okay with being selfish

Your heart is what attracts me

Love me until you're empty

He complemented all of me, heart, body & mind

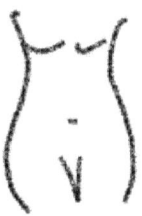

Whisper in my ear what you want me to do
I want to show you that you're mine

talking about
your feelings
turns me on

He told her everything
he wanted to do to her

Open my heart & soul
the way you open my legs

He was patient & kind to
my wandering mind

I want your lips to kiss me for eternity

There is something so special
about a mouth that does not bite

Our love is what I enjoy writing about most

their clothes on the floor
where they started by the door
their body's craving each other
their hearts thinking there could never be another

Mornings with you
Coffee for two

He was different in the simplest ways

I want to be alive
That was the first time those words
came out of the girls's mouth

His mouth impressed me in many ways

Hold your body up close & tight to mine
& tell me how much you need me

I've felt your light in the darkest places

Your eyes shining like the stars
on a full moon autumn night

Your lips drip honey & wine onto mine

You satisfy me like fresh brewed coffee
on Sunday morning

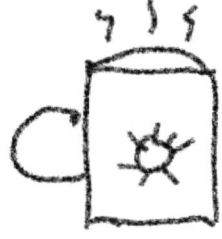

Emotionally intelligent people
are my kind of people
there is such beauty in being able
to have a raw meaningful conversation anytime

I'm finally happy to be me
The door to the past is locked & I'm finally feeling free
There seems to be new opportunities daily
I've been learning to love & understand myself lately
I enjoy the quiet mornings alone
I'm happier now that there's less on my phone

Our love sweet like homemade wine

Music playing in the kitchen
The living room windows open
Curtains are catching the breeze
The hallway a mess with laundry
ring ring
The oven saying lunch is ready
Enjoy your day

The one who is meant for you isn't going to ignore your needs
They won't just do bare minimum deeds
They'll notice what excites you most when you're talking
They'll hold your hand while walking
They'll ask about your past pets & goals
They'll cherish your soul

For once in my life I'm genuinely happy to be alive
The morning light that gets in my curtains no longer bothers me
The grocery store checkout line moving slow doesn't get to me
The rain doesn't ruin my day anymore
The drive-through messing up my order isn't the end of the world
I've been praying my life ended for so long
I will no longer allow small moments to ruin my time alive

I need you the way a bee
needs nectar from a flower

Please don't judge me
some parts are scarred
He began kissing her body slowly
showing each part love
she was in awe that a person
could be so gentle & loving

You touch me without contact

No need to go Christmas shopping
Just write me a love letter

They continue the little things throughout the whole relationship
The compliments didn't stop
The simple surprises didn't go unnoticed
The kind gestures didn't fade
Their love for each other growing every day

She was inexperienced & filled with innocence
He talked her through each moment

His mouth said he would change
his actions never said he was changing

What if we all admired ourselves
the way we admire our best friend

"The apple doesn't fall far from the tree"
I flew away from my tree

Your emotions aren't too big
You just presented them to the wrong people

Your moment hasn't passed
The sun will rise again
You can try then

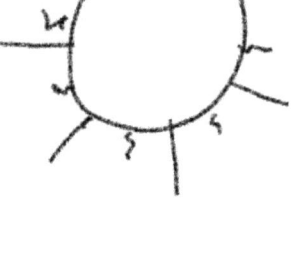

Your attempt failed for a reason

please be gentle &
patient with every part of me

I'll always be cheering you on
no matter the distance
no matter the time

Please be the one who stays

How you treat yourself
is how others treat you
Value your opinions
your time
your heart
There is no one else
like you

Go where you're wanted & celebrated
We all deserve that

You have healed my soul
Your words have healed my soul

Talk to me softly
Yelling will get you no where

The world is full of opportunities
when your eyes are open

How do you know when
you haven't given it everything

You'll know why someday
Maybe when it's too late
Or when the timing is fate

Stop asking questions you can't handle the answers too
Stop setting yourself up for pain

Sit with me anywhere
Talk to me about anything
Your presence is a gift

I am achieving my life goals
later then I planned &
that's okay because
I am achieving my life goals

It will all workout

Failing is a part of the process
Learn from it
Don't let it discourage you

Don't force a connection
We're not all meant for each other

Your voice is the sun
Your heart is the moon &
Your mind is the stars

All beautiful & admired

we talk all day
yet we still have so much to say

call me whenever &
wherever
for there is
no moment I don't
want to hear your voice

I always ran away from my problems
you made me face them
in the moment I was livid
now I thank you

Your way of living is
passionate & inspiring
I want to be
with you forever

It really did all work out
I can't believe it

I can't talk to you
if your ears are
always closed

my heart was locked for so long
it was you who had the key
you say I'm free to be me

you came so unexpectedly
for that reason it scared me
but you turned out to be the
best thing that happened to me

you're a blessing in my eyes

Please be the one who proves me wrong

You're a want & a need

Talk to me about anything
I just want to hear your voice
It calms my mind

Tell me you want me
Tell me you need me
Tell me anything

You'll fall in love at fourteen
Think your world has fallen apart at sixteen
Change your clothes hair nails
& makeup eventually
Dismiss all the advice along the way
You'll feel on top of the world at eighteen
The world has lost color at nineteen
Filled with anger & pain for a couple years
Then in your twenties it all comes together

Your name appears on my phone & the world is quiet

How to love me
get me flowers sometimes
write me letters or notes
accept my anxiety.. it's not leaving
please don't make me feel invisible

I'm free
Your words don't hurt me
Your eyes don't scare me
Your actions don't affect me
I waited 21 years for this feeling

I am healing
Thankfully I'm in the exploring
& trying new things in life stage
I love it
I have learned so much about myself
There are areas that I need to reshape
& areas I have found deserving of more love

Somehow you turn words into lyrics
Sound into song
Scraps into a whole
You leave everything better then
how you found it
If our time comes to an end
I hope I am left better then how you found me

Recommending a book is a love language

If the end is heartbreak
I'll still read our story

Love with the intentions of putting more hearts back together then adding more chipped pieces

I love my sister's beautiful blue eyes
I appreciate my friends voice
for it is smart & wise
I am grateful for my dads patient
& selfless heart
I am thankful for my friends
creative & expressive art
I have so many blessings
-Thank you

I wanted to kiss him all over
Especially the broken parts

His hands around my waist
our mouths anything but talking
sin in the air
my hands in his hair
the night lingers on
like his hands down my waist
tracing every imperfect curve

"Wow that's a beautiful name how do you spell that"

My clothes were on the floor

I never believed "the days will get better"s
My days were dark for so long
I forgot how the light felt
I don't remember much of my teenage years
They were swallowed by depression
My mind highjacked in a constant state of
misery rage & confusion
If you're reading this in the dark
If your mind is highjacked
Know it really does get better
Believe me please & keep going

www.ingramcontent.com/pod-product-compliance
Lightning Source LLC
Chambersburg PA
CBHW032103090426
42743CB00007B/216